ZONDER**kidz**™   # I Can Read!™   2 WITH HELP

DAVID
and God's Giant Victory

pictures by Dennis G. Jones

A long time ago, the Israelite army
and the Philistine army
were ready to fight.
There was a very big man
in the Philistine army.

His name was Goliath.

Goliath was nine feet tall.

He was very, very strong.

The Israelite army was filled

with fear!

David's brothers were in the

Israelite army.

Their father, Jesse, told David

to bring them food.

David went to check on his

brothers too.

David brought food to his brothers.

He heard Goliath dare the Israelites

to send a man to fight with him.

Goliath shouted, "Choose one of

your men to face me!"

No one stepped forward.

The Israelite army was scared.

But David was not scared!

He trusted God to keep him safe.

"Who does Goliath think he is?"

asked David.

Saul, the Israelite king,

heard about David.

He was surprised by what he heard.

"Let me go fight Goliath,"
David said to King Saul.
The king said, "David,
you are too small.
You cannot fight that giant!"

But David knew God would
keep him safe.
He fought a lion and a bear to
protect his father's sheep!
David trusted God to help him.

"Go and fight the giant.

God be with you,"

King Saul said to David.

Then he gave David his armor,

helmet, and a sword.

But everything was too big

for David to use.

David took the armor off.

He left Saul's sword on the ground.

He knew he could win the fight

with Goliath.

David had a plan.

David trusted God to keep him safe.

He prayed to God for strength.

Then David took his slingshot,

and he went to a stream.

David looked all around the stream.

He chose five smooth stones

for his slingshot.

He put them in his

shepherd's bag.

David was ready!

David approached the giant man
named Goliath.

He was not scared at all.

Even when Goliath looked at him

with anger,

David was not afraid.

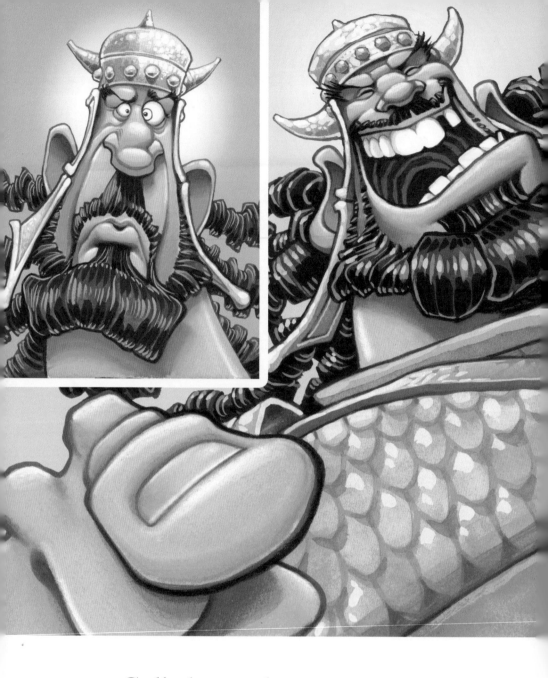

Goliath saw that

David was young and small.

He was surprised that this boy

would try to fight him.

David said, "Today the world will know
there is a great God in Israel."
He got his slingshot and stone ready.

David whirled it.

David twirled it.

Goliath watched and was not happy.

Whoosh!

David slung the stone at Goliath.

The stone hit Goliath

on the head, and he fell down.

David did not need a sword,

a spear, or armor.

David only needed God's help.

David won the battle against Goliath!

David was right—

the battle belonged to the Lord!

He struck Goliath down

with just a slingshot and a stone —

and God's great love!